··* AlphaTales *·*·*
A to Z Letter Formation
Practice Pages

Fun-Filled Reproducible Practice Pages That Help Young Learners
Recognize and Print Every Letter of the Alphabet

SCHOLASTIC
PROFESSIONAL BOOKS

New York • Toronto • London • Auckland • Sydney • New Delhi
Mexico City • Hong Kong • Buenos Aires

Cover by Kelli Thompson, interior design by Norma Ortiz

ISBN: 0-439-33151-X

Contents

Introduction

The Practice Sheets

Teaching Letter Formation with AlphaTales

Welcome to AlphaTales: A to Z Letter Formation Practice Pages! These ready-to-go pages introduce and reinforce each letter's upper- and lowercase formation. They also ensure kids get lots of practice with the featured letter—all with the help of friendly AlphaTales creatures!

Research shows that automatic letter recognition is a critical element for reading success. Kids need to be able to read their own writing—and that of others! Though they will naturally develop their own handwriting style as they become more confident, fluent writers, all kids need to learn the basic strokes (and sequence of strokes) involved in each letter's formation. In this way, copying rows of letters reinforces the shape of each letter and provides visual and kinesthetic reinforcement.

In addition to letter formation practice, the pages provide an opportunity for kids to develop phonemic awareness.

Each letter is introduced by a familiar AlphaTale animal whose name begins with the target letter, and alliterative sentences from all 26 AlphaTales stories highlight initial sounds.

In addition to using the pages for explicit, whole group instruction, you might:

- send blank pages home with children to practice at home

- put copies of the pages in the writing center

- have children create alphabet folders in which they put their completed sheets and bind into a book when all 26 sheets have been completed

- include the sheets in children's portfolios

Using the Practice Sheets in Your Classroom

With these practice sheets, children experience each letter in a variety of ways. Children will:

- trace letters and form their own letters

- discriminate between similar letters

- recognize and copy letters that represent initial sounds

- develop a sight word vocabulary

- play with alliterative sentences

Practice rows guide children in the formation of each letter, first by tracing and then by writing on their own. Numbered arrows demonstrate the sequence of strokes involved, while plenty of write-on lines provide lots of room for writing practice.

A letter hunt helps children discriminate between commonly confused letters, building faster letter recognition. Children then count the number of target letters they circled.

Alliterative sentences allow children to use the target letter while examining and recognizing initial sounds. Children first trace the initial letters, then try writing the letters by themselves.

Word squares present simple words and pictures that help build sight word vocabulary and additional awareness of initial sounds.

Procedures for Letter Practice

You might follow these five steps for each letter practice sheet:

1. Preview the letter you will introduce by writing it on the board or chart paper. Then give each child a sheet. Ask them to name the animal they see at the top.

2. Together, examine the letter children will be practicing. Again demonstrate the letter on the board and narrate its formation ("The letter a starts at the top, with a circle, then a stick straight down").

3. Have children "air trace" the letter in the air.

4. Children can then trace and write the letters on the lines using pencil. Point out the numbers and arrows. You might say the numbers aloud as children trace the first letter.

5. Have children complete one row of the letter, compare it to the model, and then circle their best letter in the row.

Beyond the Practice Sheets

Extend letter practice beyond the practice sheets and let children experience letters in a variety of ways! Involve all the senses with these ideas:

- Get messy! Let children use their fingers to trace letters in thin layers of shaving cream, fingerpaint, pudding, or whipped cream. Tape a large piece of waxed paper to desks and spread the messy material thin. Then invite children to "write" with their index finger!

- Get tactile. Have children trace letters in sand—put damp sand in a shallow tray and have children use their fingers to form letters. Or, use a damp sponge to practice letters on the blackboard (the letters will disappear as they dry)!

- Have children form letters with their bodies (children may do this alone or in small groups).

- "Talk through" the formation of each letter, describing the various strokes and shapes. Auditory learners will benefit from this sort of narration.

- Have pairs of children trace letter shapes onto each other's backs and hands. The child "receiving" the letter tries to guess which letter was formed.

- Set up a "letter center" with letter magnets, letter stamps, letter sponges, alphabet-shaped pasta, paper and writing supplies, and so on.

Name _____

✱ Trace and write.

A is for Alligator.

A A

a a

✱ Circle every A and every a.

A	A	E	A	O	E	A	E
o	e	a	O	a	a	O	e	o	a

I found _____ A's and _____ a's.

Name _____

✷ Trace the A's and a's.

A l l i g a t o r p a i n t s a n a p p l e.

✷ Now write the A's and a's.

_ l l i g a t o r p a i n t s _ n _ p p l e.

✷ Add a's and then read the words.

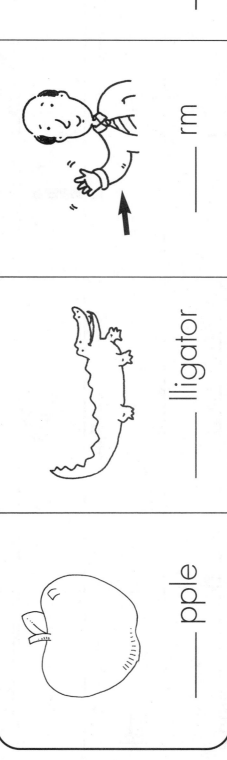

_ pple

_ lligator

_ _ rm

Now draw and write your own **Aa** word.

_____

Name _____

✿ Trace and write.

B is for Bear.

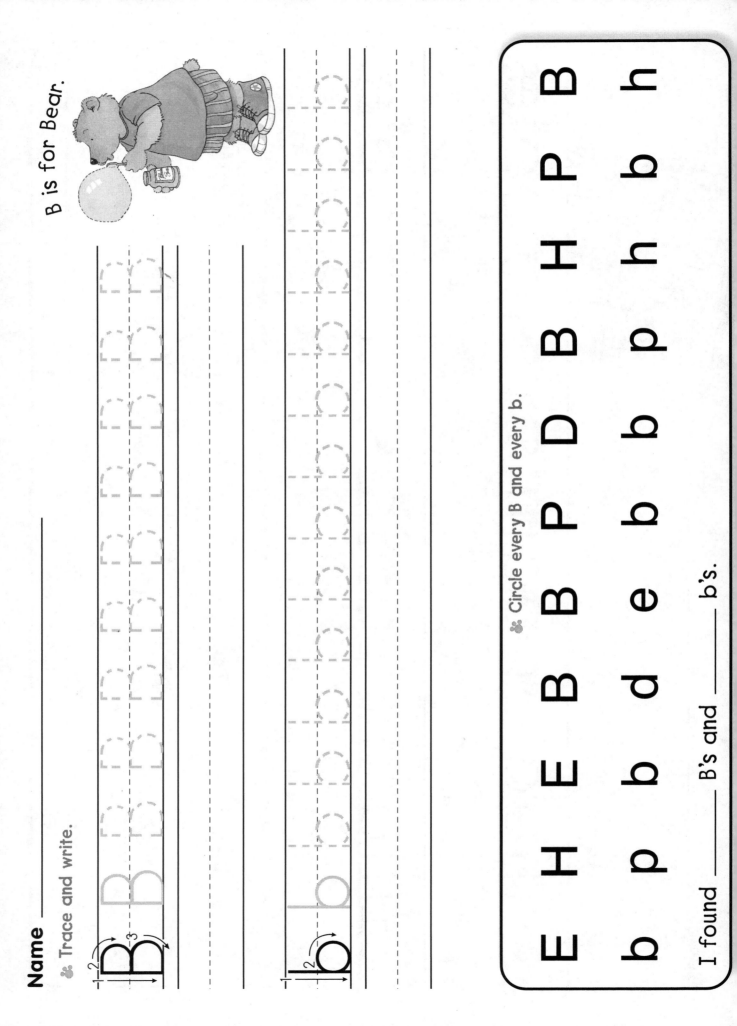

B B B

b

✿ Circle every B and every b.

E	H	B	B	D	B	H	P	B
b	p	b	d	e	b	b	p	h

I found _____ B's and _____ b's.

Name _____

✱ Trace the B's and b's.

Bubble Bear blows bubbles.

✱ Now write the B's and b's.

_____ubble _____ear _____lows _____ubbles.

✱ Add b's and then read the words.

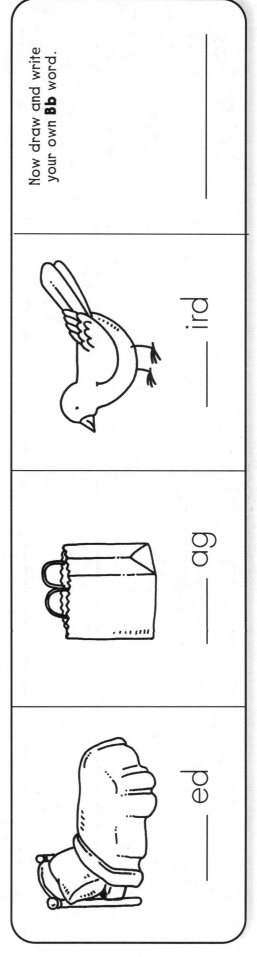

_____ed   _____ag   _____ird

Now draw and write your own **Bb** word.

_____

Name _____

✿ Trace and write.

C is for Cats.

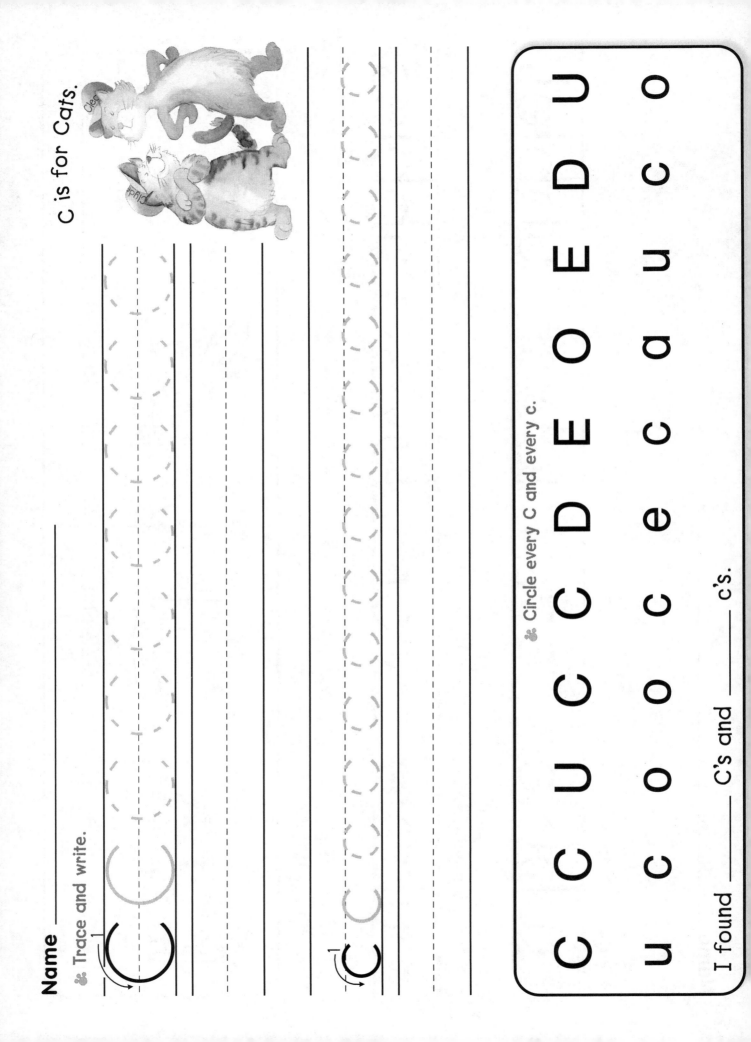

✿ Circle every C and every c.

| C | C | U | C | D | E | O | D | U |

| u | c | o | o | c | e | c | a | u | o |

I found _____ C's and _____ c's.

Name _____

✺ Trace the C's and c's.

Cleo Carries cocoa.

✺ Now write the C's and c's.

_leo _arries _ocoa.

✺ Add c's and then read the words.

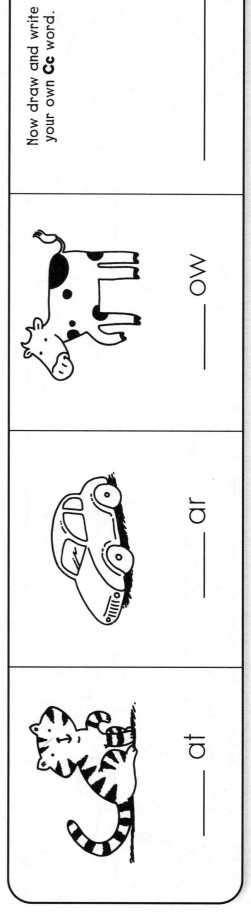

_____ at

_____ ar

_____ ow

Now draw and write your own **Cc** word.

_____

Name _____

🐾 Trace and write.

D is for Dog

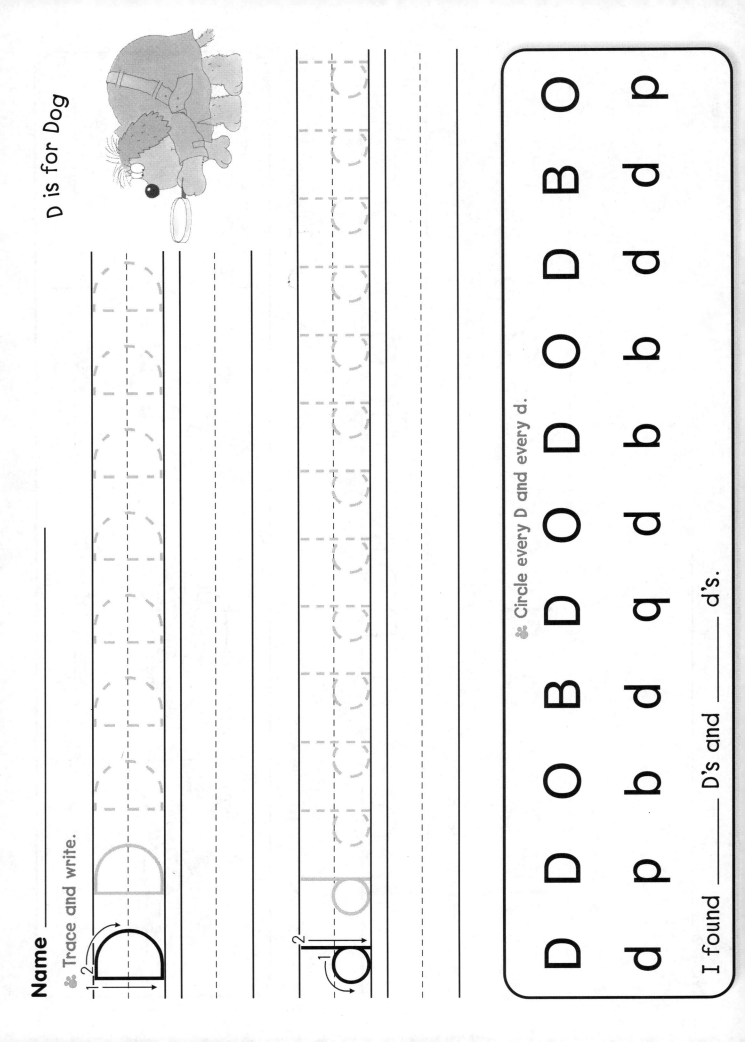

🐾 Circle every D and every d.

D	D	O	B	D	B	O
d	p	b	q	O	d	p
p	b	q	d	b	b	d

I found _____ D's and _____ d's.

Name _____

❧ Trace the D's and d's.

Detective Dog likes doughnuts.

❧ Now write the D's and d's.

_____etective _____og likes _____oughnuts.

❧ Add d's and then read the words.

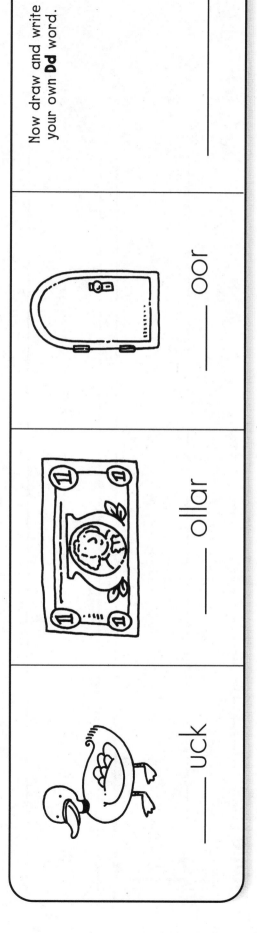

_____ uck

_____ ollar

_____ oor

Now draw and write your own **Dd** word.

_____

Name _____

✐ Trace and write.

E is for Elephant.

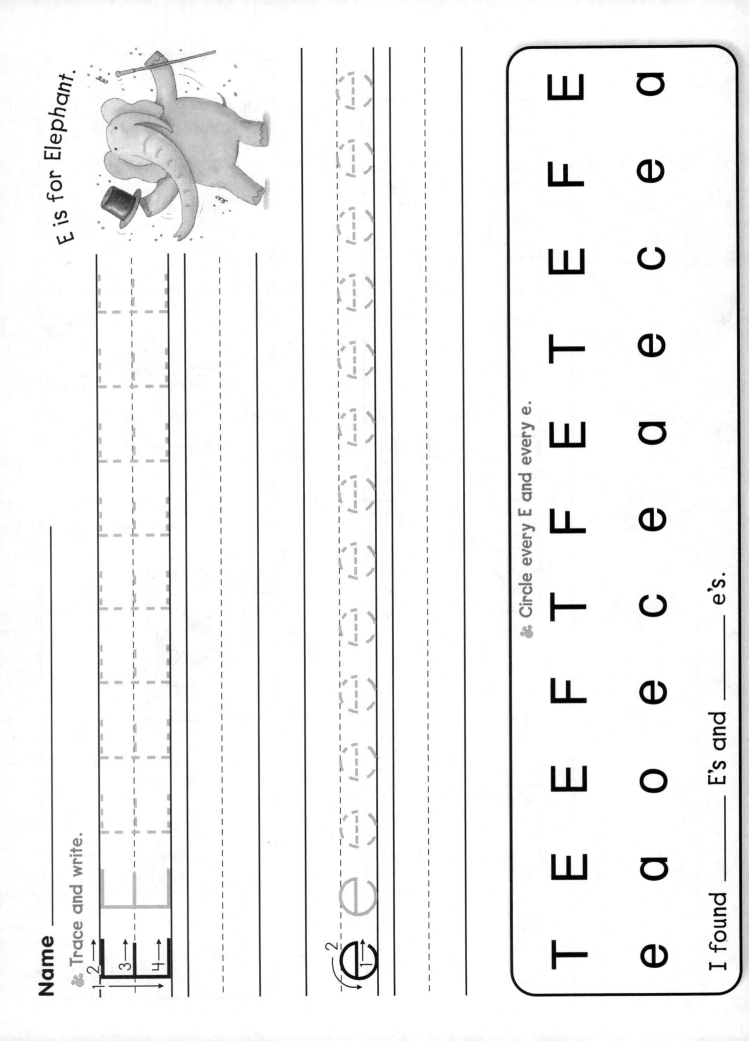

✐ Circle every E and every e.

T   E   E   F   T   F   E   T

e   a   o   e   c   e   a

I found _____ E's and _____ e's.

Name _____

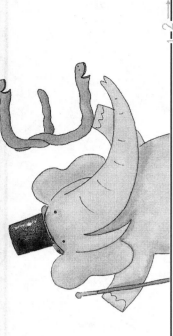

✿ Trace the E's.

E̲ ̲v̲in the E̲ ̲ ̲lephant makes an E̲ ̲.

✿ Now write the E's.

_____ vin the _____ lephant makes an _____.

✿ Add e's and then read the words.

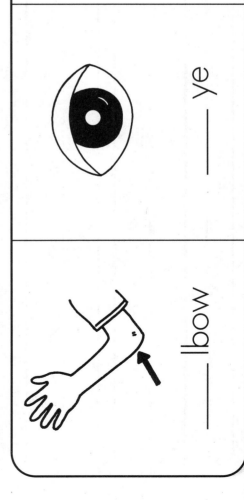

_____ lbow   _____ ye   _____ gg

Now draw and write your own **Ee** word.

_____

Name _____

✂ Trace and write.

F is for Ferret.

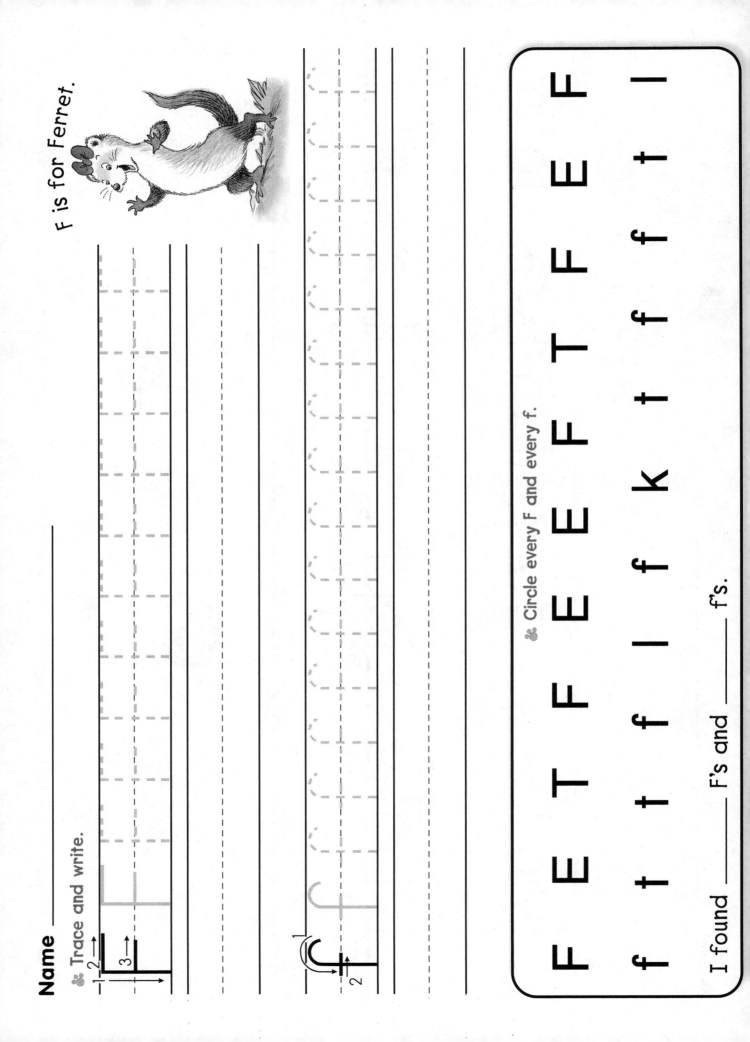

✂ Circle every F and every f.

F E T F F T T F F E F

f t f f I f k t f f t

I found _____ F's and _____ f's.

Name _____

❧ Trace the F's and f's.

F ifi the F erret plays the f lute.

❧ Now write the F's and f's.

____ ifi the ____ erret plays the ____ lute.

❧ Add f's and then read the words.

____ eather

____ ish

____ ork

Now draw and write your own **Ff** word.

____

Name _____

  ✎ Trace and write.

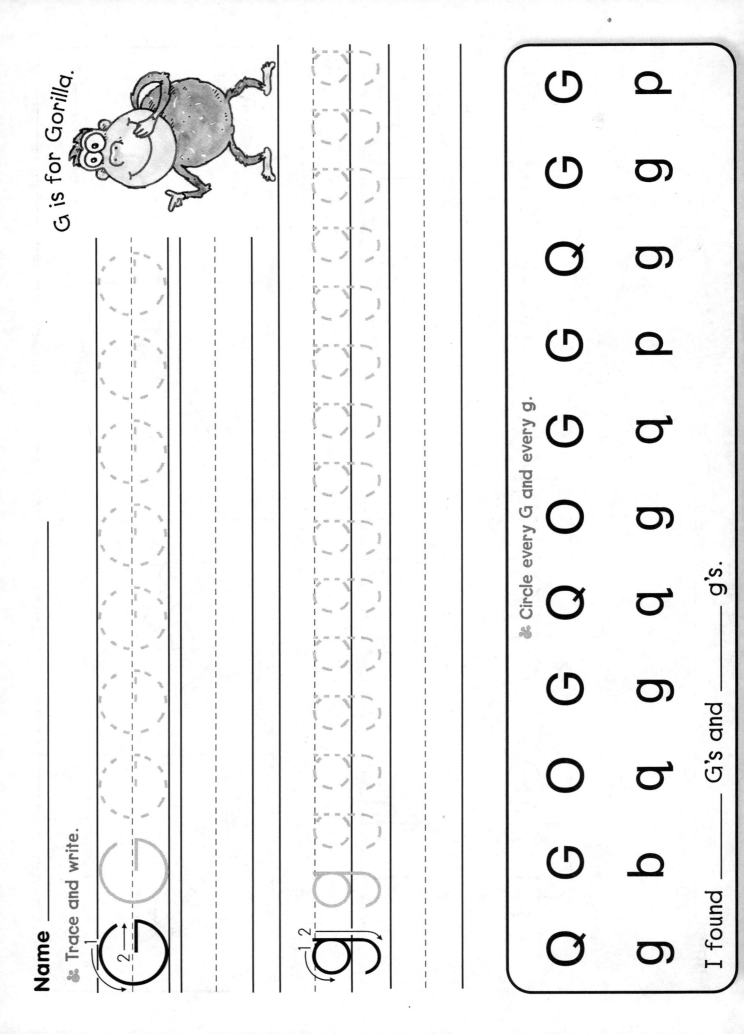

G is for Gorilla.

✎ Circle every G and every g.

Q	G	O	G	G	G	G
G	O	G	O	Q	G
g	q	g	q	g	q	p
b	q	g	q	g	g	p

I found _____ G's and _____ g's.

Name _____

❧ Trace the G's and g's.

Gorilla gobbles gooseberries.

❧ Now write the G's and g's.

_____orilla _____obbles _____ooseberries.

❧ Add g's and then read the words.

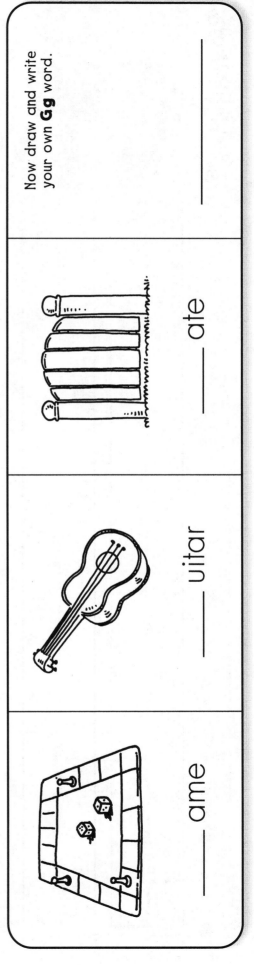

_____ame

_____uitar

_____ate

Now draw and write your own **Gg** word.

_____

Name _____

H is for Hippopotamus.

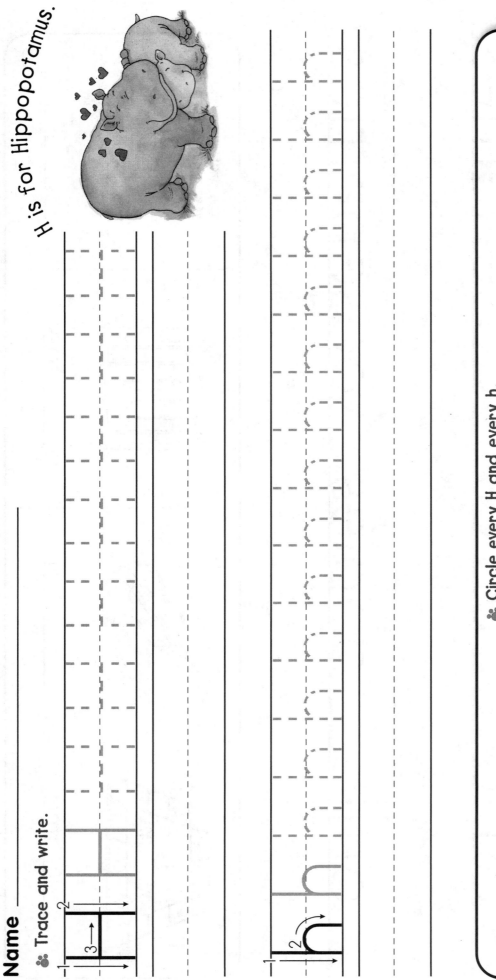

❦ Trace and write.

❦ Circle every H and every h.

| T | H | H | T | H | L | I | H | Y |

| b | h | I | p | h | I | h | I | b |

I found _____ H's and _____ h's.

Name _____

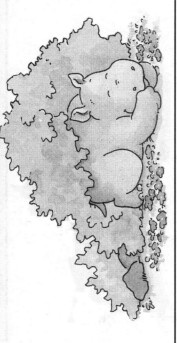

❧ Trace the H and h.

H|ippo is hiding.

❧ Now write the H and h.

|ippo is ____iding.

❧ Add h's and then read the words.

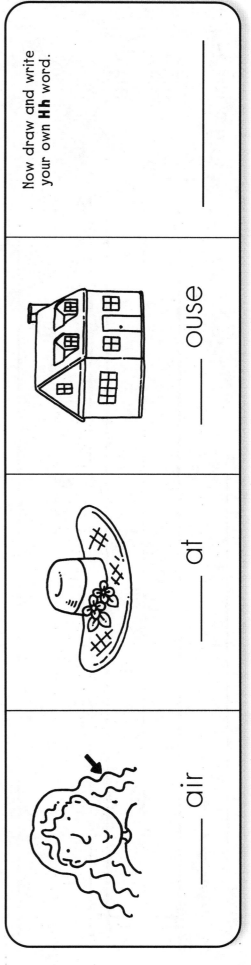

____ouse

____at

____air

Now draw and write your own **Hh** word.

_____

Name _____

I is for Iguana.

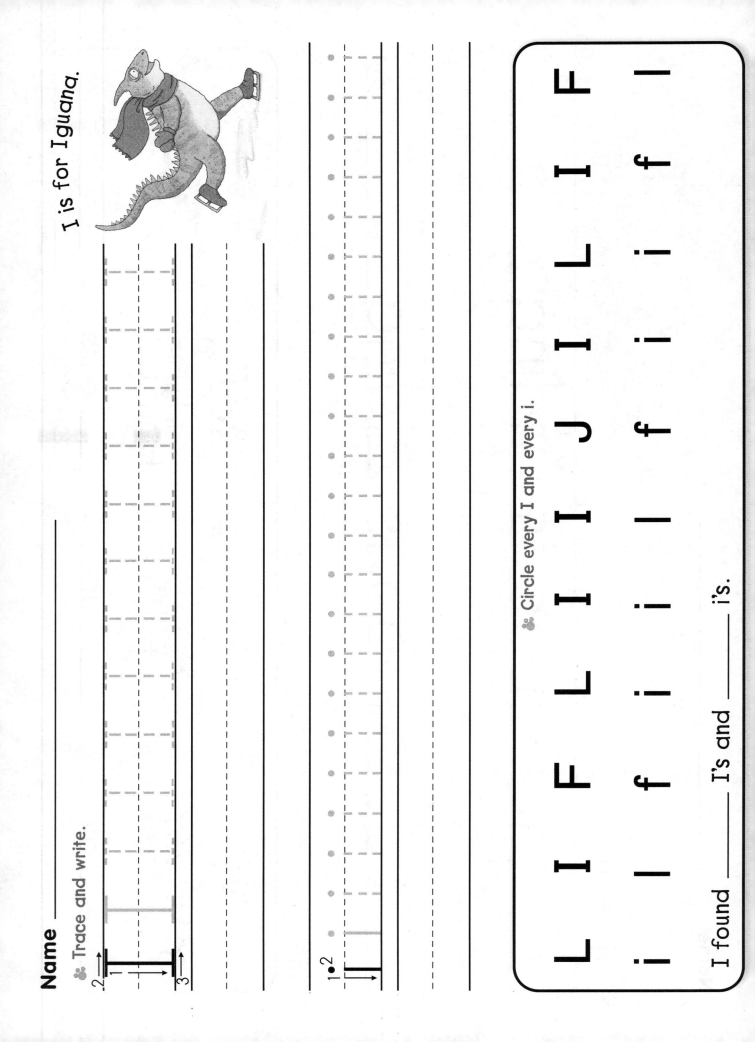

Trace and write.

2↑ ‖3↑

1•2

Circle every I and every i.

L   I   F   L   I   J   I   L   I   F

i   f   I   i   l   f   i   f   i   f

I found _____ I's and _____ i's.

Name _____

❧ Trace the I's and i's.

I guana I's on an iceberg.

❧ Now write the I's and i's.

_____ guana _____s on an _____ceberg.

❧ Add i's and then read the words.

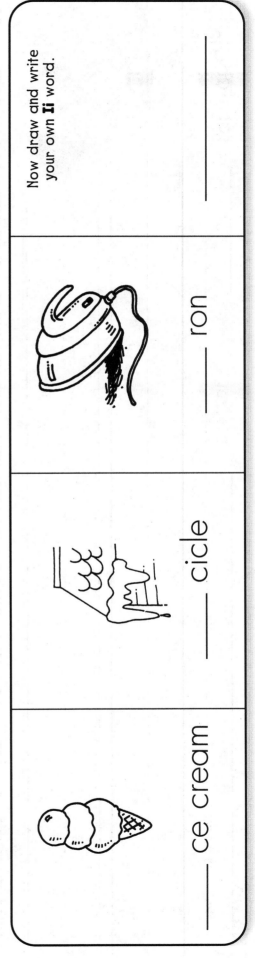

_____ce cream   _____cicle   _____ron

Now draw and write your own **Ii** word.

_____

Name _____

Trace and write.

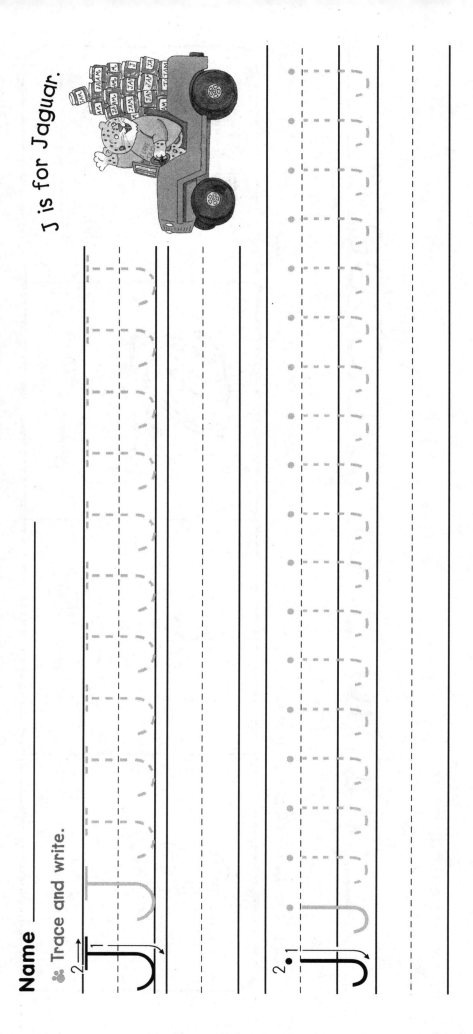

J is for Jaguar.

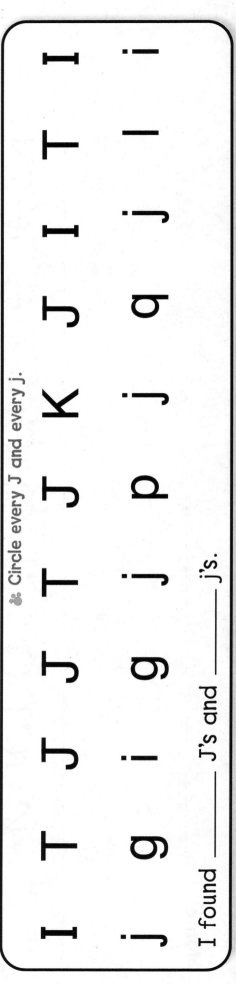

I found _____ J's and _____ j's.

Name _____

✿ Trace the J and j.

J aguar loves j am.

✿ Now write the J and j.

_____ aguar loves _____ am.

✿ Add j's and then read the words.

_____ ar

_____ ump

_____ eans

Now draw and write your own **Jj** word.

_____

Name _____

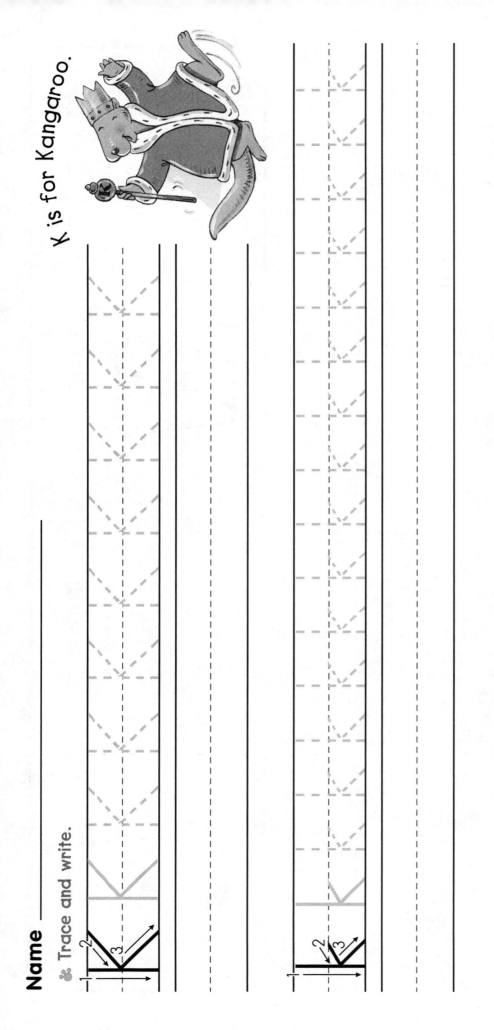

✎ Trace and write.

K is for Kangaroo.

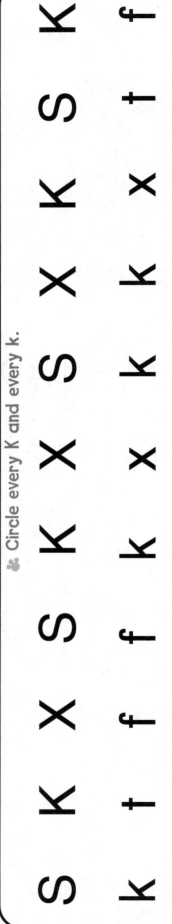

✿ Circle every K and every k.

S	K	X	S	K	X	K	S	K
k	t	f	f	k	x	k	x	f

I found _____ K's and _____ k's.

Name _____

❧ Trace the K and k.

$\underline{K}$angaroo plays $\underline{k}$ azoo.

❧ Now write the K and k.

____ angaroo plays ____ azoo.

❧ Add k's and then read the words.

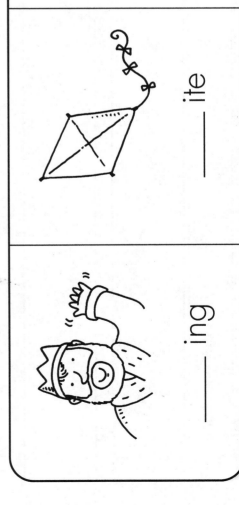

____ing

____ite

____angaroo

Now draw and write your own **Kk** word.

____

Name _____

✿ Trace and write.

L is for Lamb.

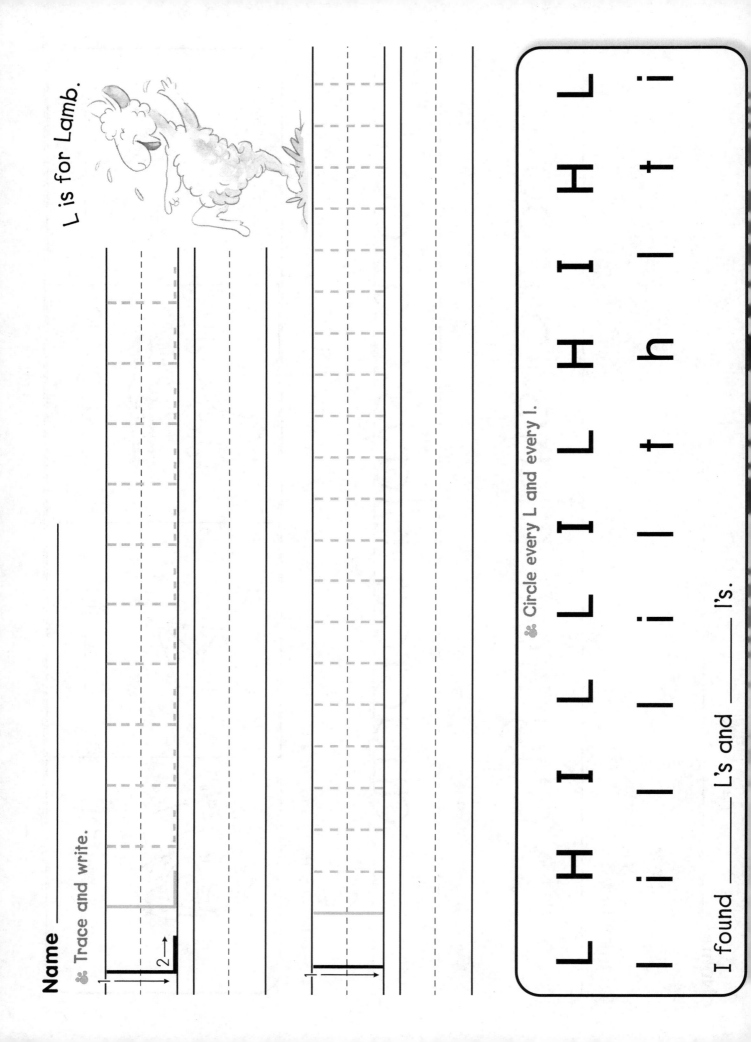

✿ Circle every L and every l.

L H I L L L H L H
l I l i I l t h i

I found _____ L's and _____ l's.

Name _____

Trace the L's and I's.

Lamb loves to laugh.

Now write the L's and I's.

_____amb _____oves to _____augh.

Add I's and then read the words.

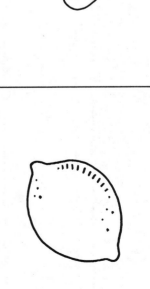
_____ emon

_____ eaf

_____ ion

Now draw and write your own **Ll** word.

_____

Name _____

Trace and write.

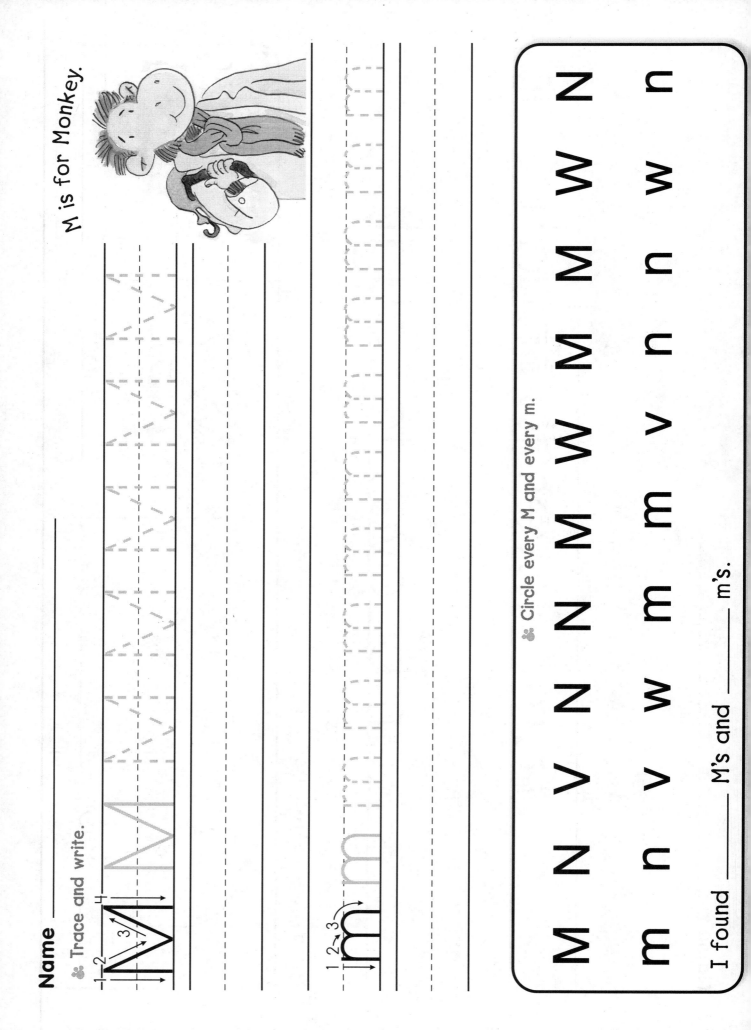

M is for Monkey.

❀ Circle every M and every m.

M	N	V	N	M	M	M	M	W
m	n	v	w	m	m	m	v	n

I found _____ M's and _____ m's.

Name _____

✎ Trace the M's and m's.

M onkey   m ops   m ilk.

✎ Now write the M's and m's.

_____ onkey   _____ ops   _____ ilk.

✎ Add m's and then read the words.

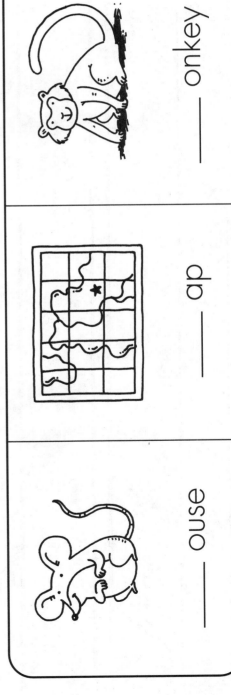

_____ ouse   _____ ap   _____ onkey

Now draw and write your own **Mm** word.

Name _____

✎ Trace and write.

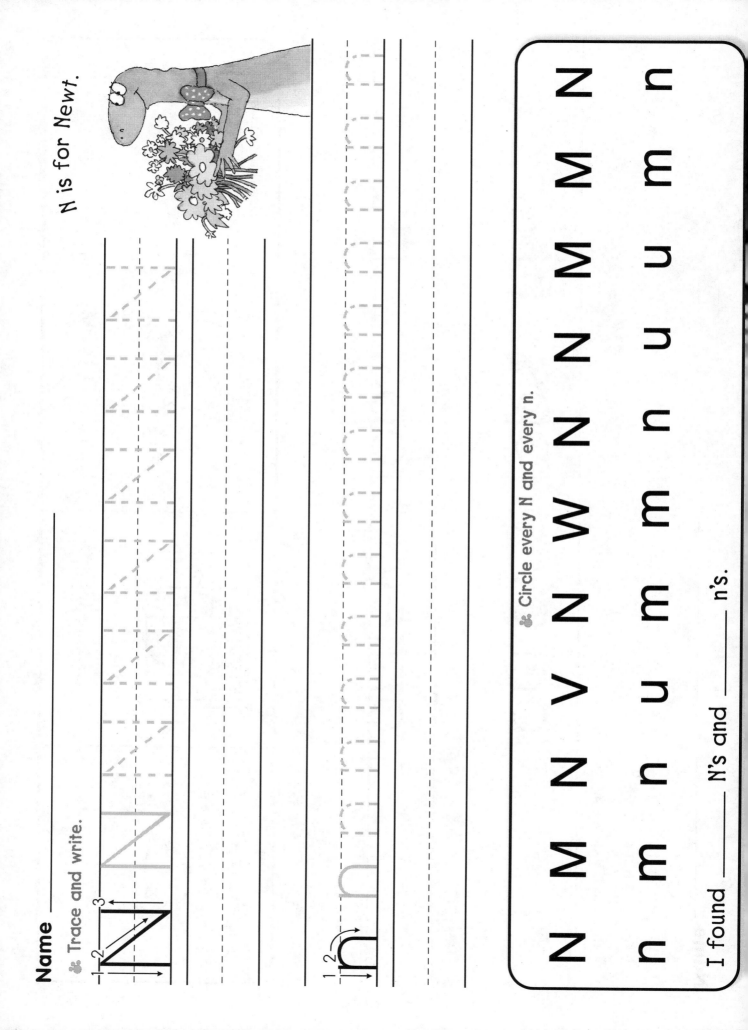

N is for *Newt.*

✎ Circle every N and every n.

N	M	N	V	N	W	N	M	N
n	m	n	u	n	m	m	u	n

I found _____ N's and _____ n's.

Name _____

❋ Trace the N's and n's.

Nate the Newt has a nickel.

❋ Now write the N's and n's.

_____ate the _____ewt has a _____ickel.

❋ Add n's and then read the words.

_____est

_____ewspaper

_____ut

Now draw and write your own **Nn** word.

_____

Name _____

✏ Trace and write.

O is for Octopus.

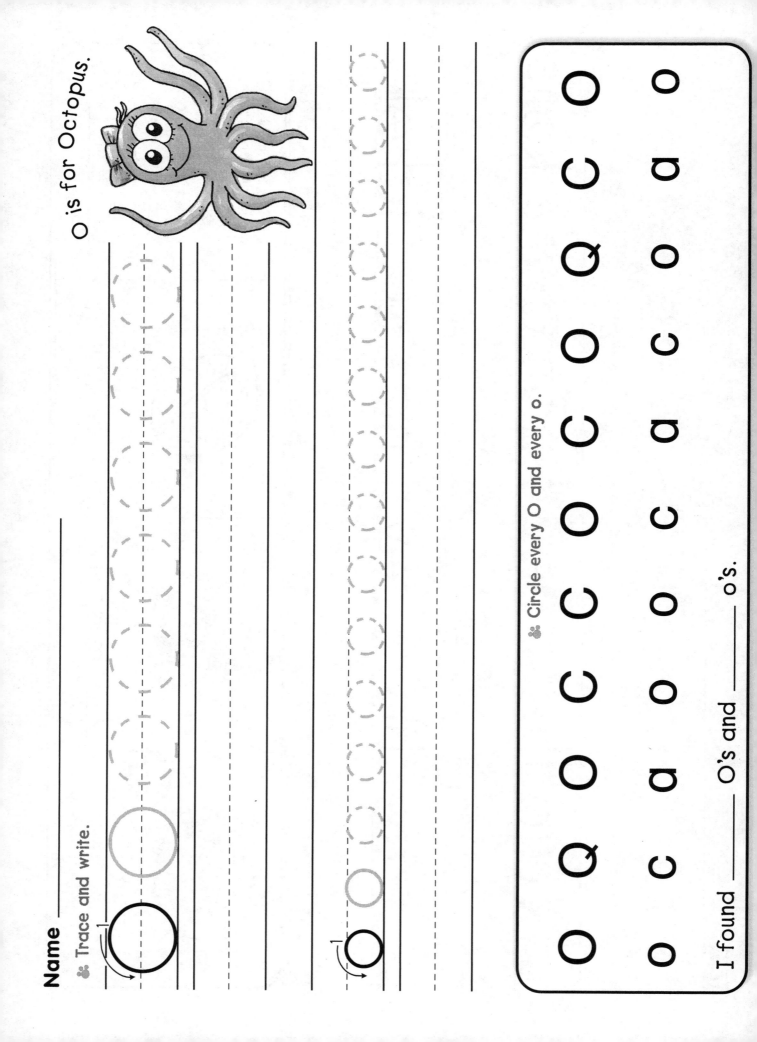

✏ Circle every O and every o.

| O | O | Q | O | C | O | C | C | C | O | O |
| o | c | a | o | o | c | o | a | c | c | a | o |

I found _____ O's and _____ o's.

Name _____

✻ Trace the O's and o's.

Olive the octopus loves onions.

✻ Now write the O's and o's.

_____ live the _____ ctopus loves _____ nions.

✻ Add o's and then read the words.

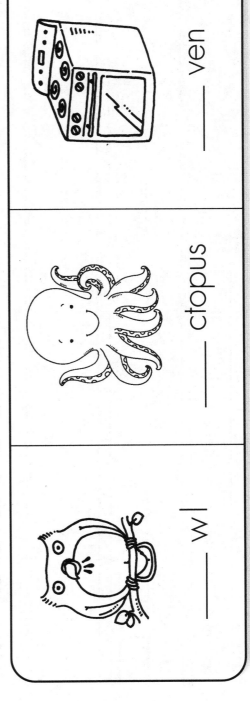

_____ wl

_____ ctopus

_____ ven

Now draw and write your own **Oo** word.

_____

Name _____

✎ Trace and write.

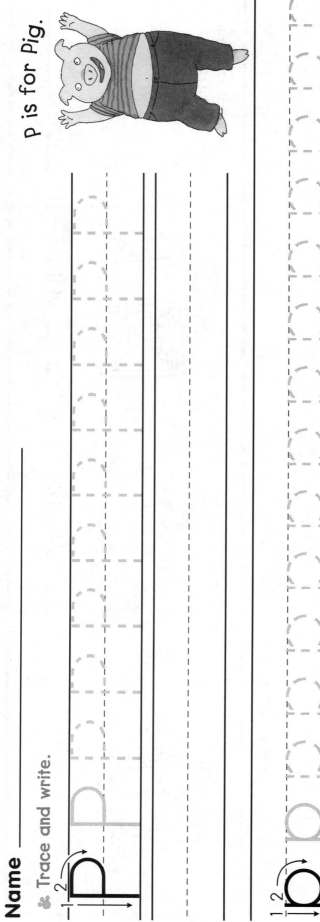

P is for Pig.

✿ Circle every P and every p.

P	R	P	B	R	P	P
R	q	p	b	d	q	p
p	q	b	p	b	p	p

I found _____ P's and _____ p's.

Name _____

❀ Trace the p's.

The pigs planned a picnic.

❀ Now write ps.

The __igs __lanned a __icnic.

❀ Add p's and then read the words.

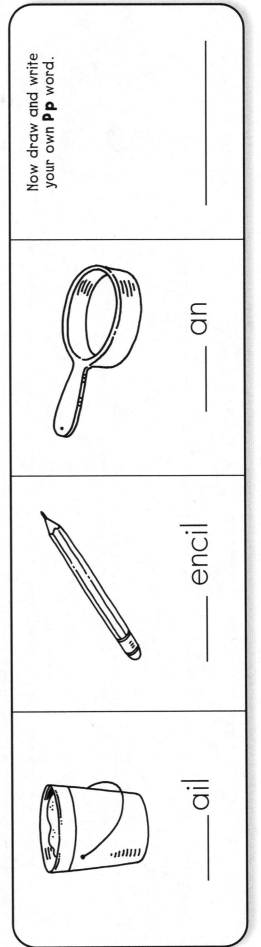

Now draw and write your own **Pp** word.

_____

____ an

____ encil

____ ail

Name _____

✿ Trace and write.

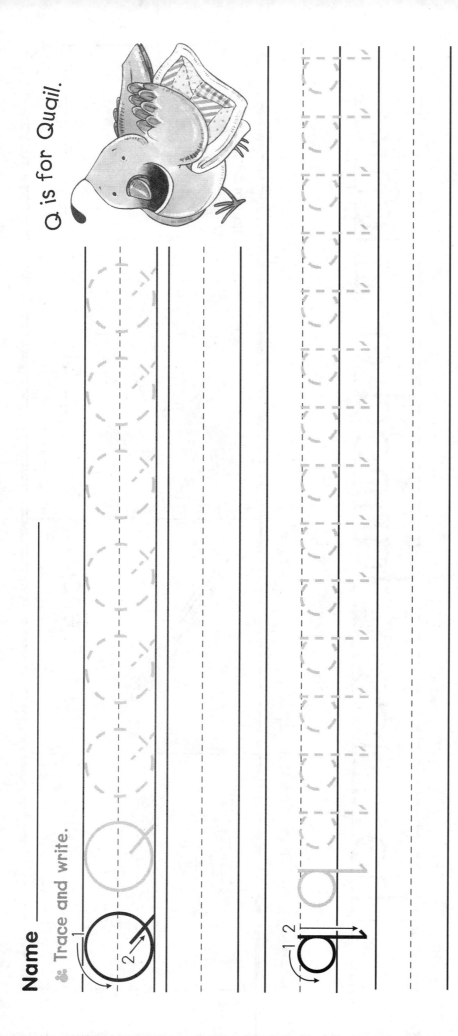

Q is for Quail.

✿ Circle every Q and every q.

Q	C	O	Q	C	O	Q
q	g	p	Q	O	C	Q
q	g	g	b	p	q	q
q	p	b	g	q	p	g

I found _____ Q's and _____ q's.

Name _____

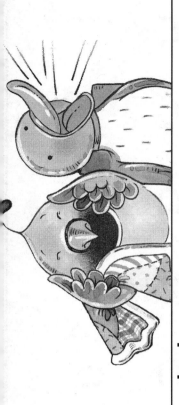

✎ Trace the Q's and q's.

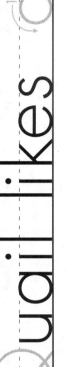

Quincy Quail likes quiet.

✎ Now write the Q's and q's.

_____ uincy _____ uail likes _____ uiet.

✎ Add q's and then read the words.

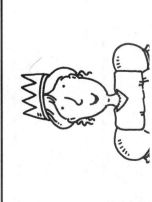

_____ ueen

_____ uilt

_____ uiet

Now draw and write
your own **Q q** word.

_____

Name _____

✿ Trace and write.

R is for Rabbit.

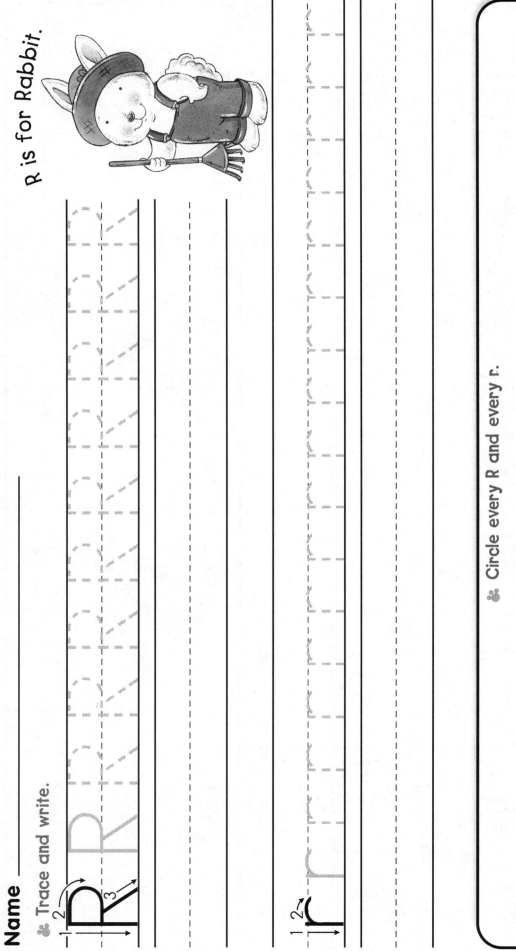

R R R

r r r

✿ Circle every R and every r.

R B P R R R B P B P R

r t n i r r t n r

I found _____ R's and _____ r's.

Name _____

❧ Trace the R's and r's.

Rosie Rabbit rakes rocks.

❧ Now write the R's and r's.

_osie _abbit _akes _ocks.

❧ Add r's and then read the words.

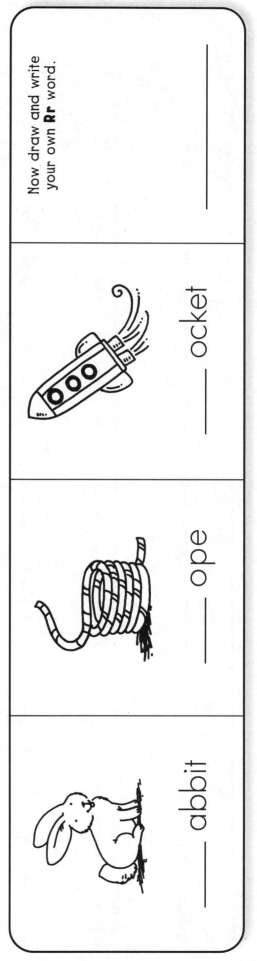

____ abbit

____ ope

____ ocket

Now draw and write your own **Rr** word.

_____

Name _____

✷ Trace and write.

s is for Seal.

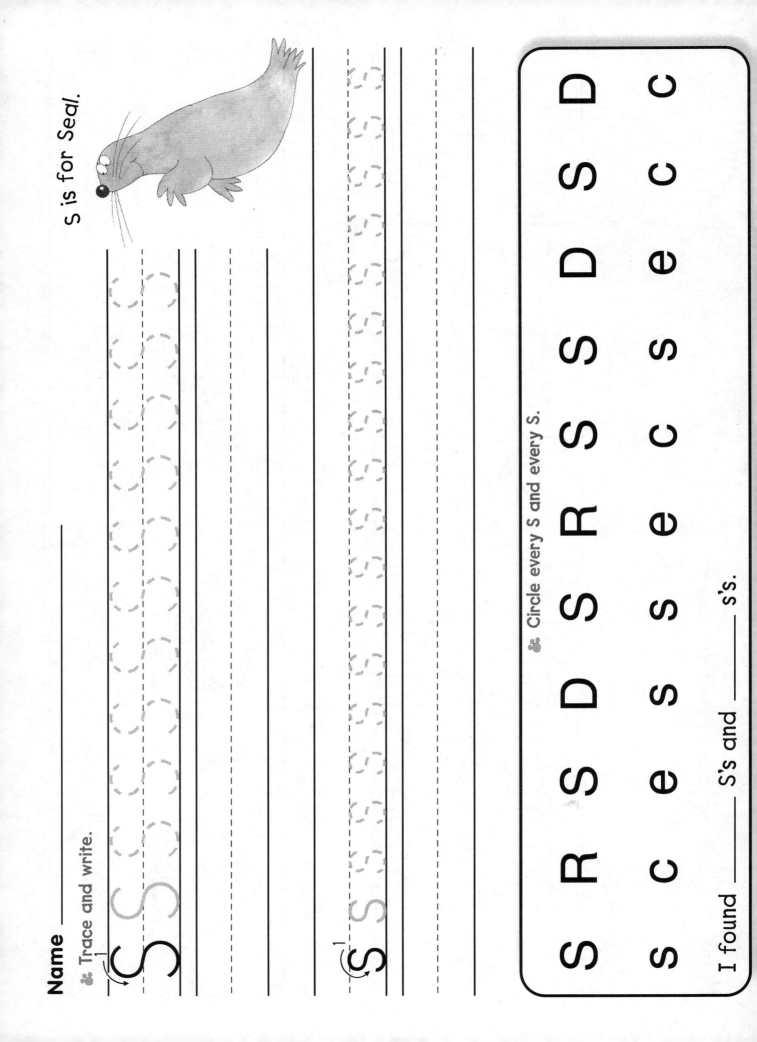

S S

S S

✷ Circle every S and every s.

S	R	S	D	S	D
s	c	e	s	e	c
S	D	S	R	S	D
s	c	e	s	c	c

I found _____ S's and _____ s's.

Name ______________________

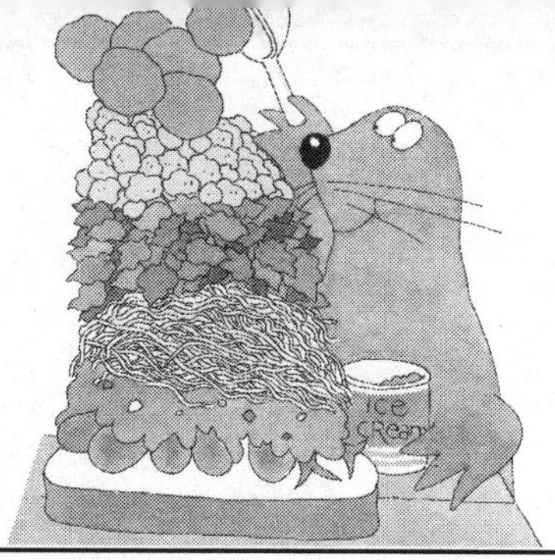

Trace the S and s.

Seal makes a sandwich.

Now write the S and s.

_eal makes a _andwich.

Add s's and then read the words.

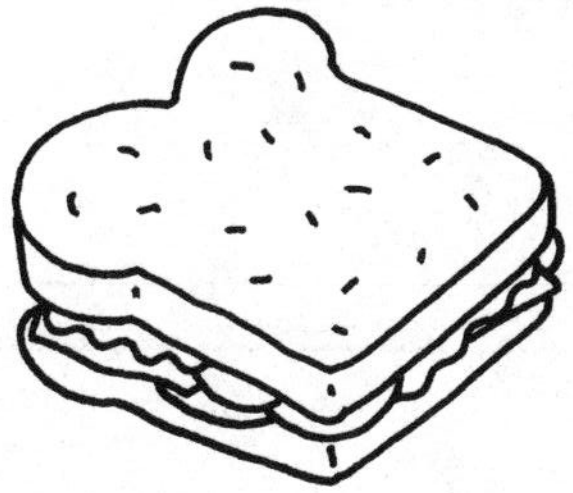	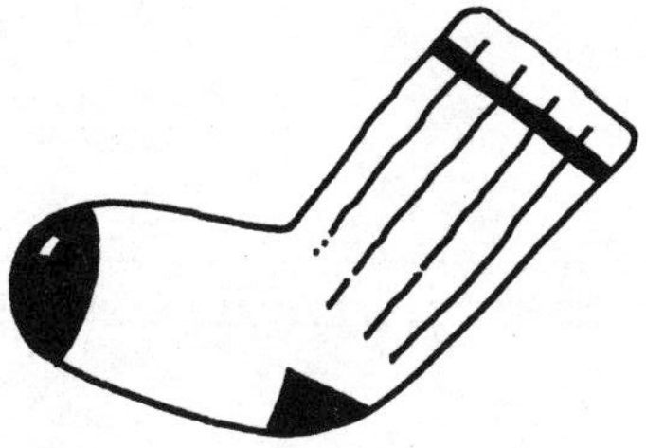	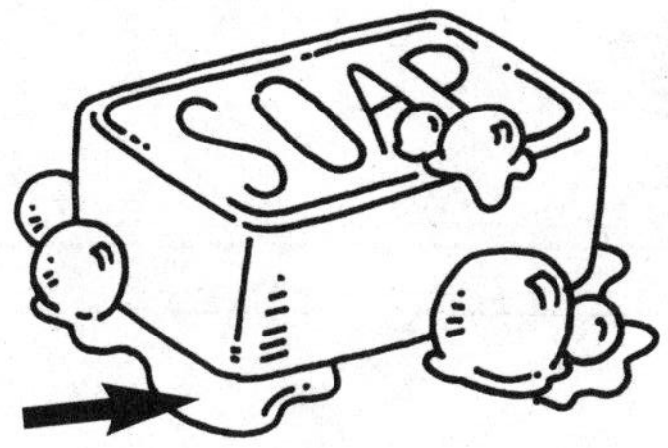	Now draw and write your own **Ss** word.
____ andwich	____ ock	____ oap	__________

Name _____

✂ Trace and write.

T is for Turtle.

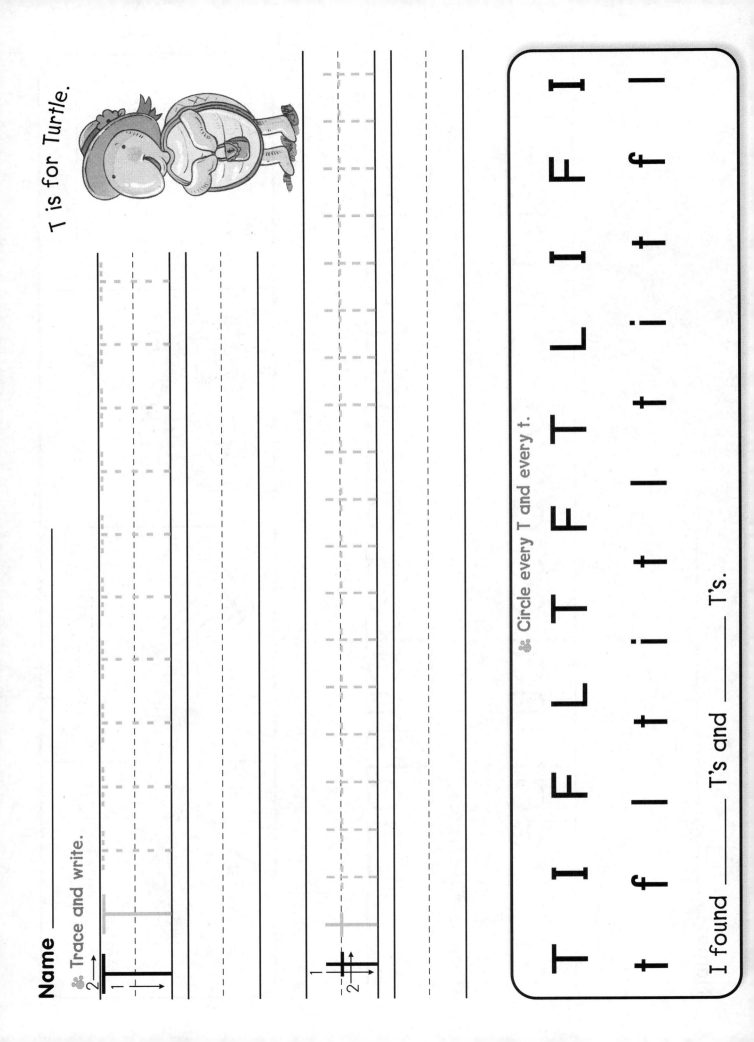

✿ Circle every T and every t.

T	I	F	L	T	F	T	L	I	F	I
t	f	t	i	t	f	I	t	i	f	l

I found _____ T's and _____ T's.

Name _____

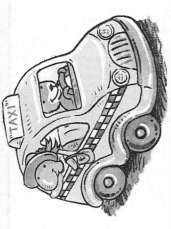

❧ Trace the T's and t's.

Tilly Turtle takes a taxi.

❧ Now write the T's and t's.

_illy _urtle _akes a _axi.

❧ Add t's and then read the words.

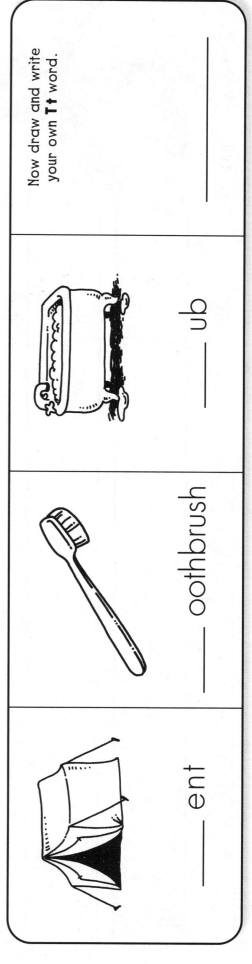

____ent

____oothbrush

____ub

Now draw and write your own **T t** word.

____

Name _____

✎ Trace and write.

U is for Umbrellabird.

UUUUUUUUU

uuuuuuuuuuuu

✿ Circle every U and every u.

C U V C O V U O U V

u c n u y u u y c n

I found _____ U's and _____ u's.

Name _____

❧ Trace the U and u.

Umbrellabird rides a unicycle.

❧ Now write the U and u.

___mbrellabird rides a _nicycle.

❧ Add u's and then read the words.

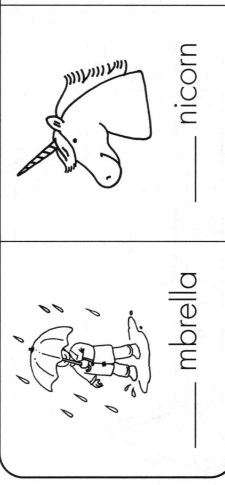

____mbrella   ____nicorn   ____p

Now draw and write your own **Uu** word.

_____

Name _____

☙ Trace and write.

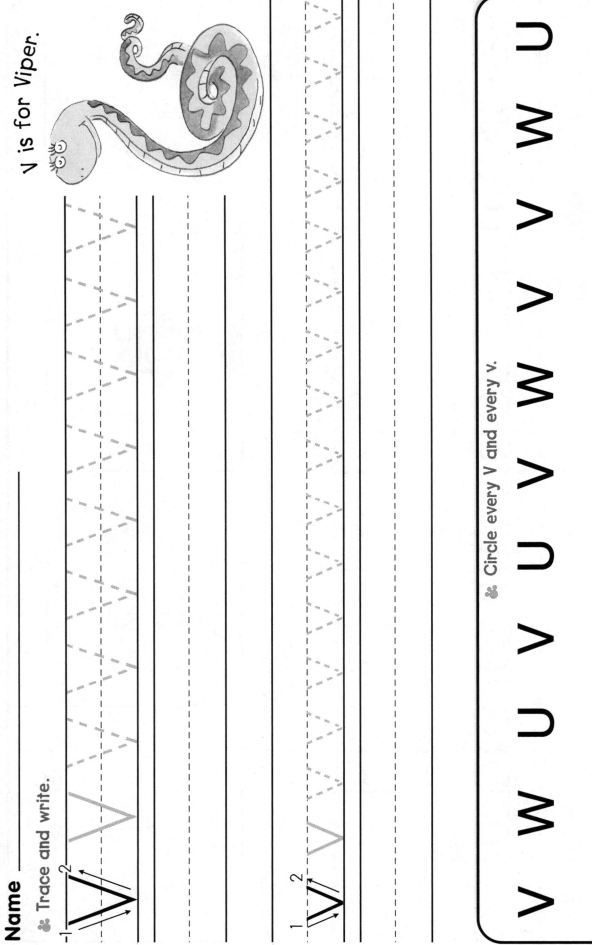

V is for Viper.

☙ Circle every V and every v.

| V | W | U | V | U | V | W | V | V | V | W | U |
| v | u | v | v | v | w | u | v | w | v | v | v |

I found _____ V's and _____ v's.

Name _____

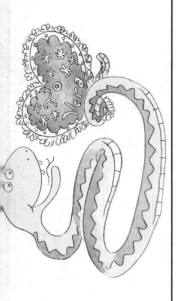

❧ Trace the V's and v's.

Vera Viper has a Valentine.

❧ Now write the V's and v's.

_____era _____iper has a _____alentine.

❧ Add v's and then read the words.

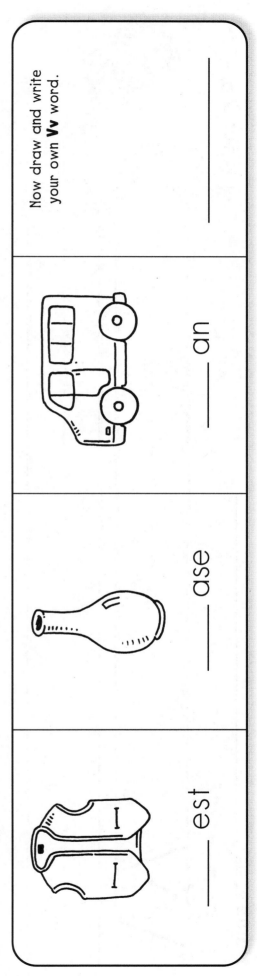

_____est

_____ase

_____an

Now draw and write your own **Vv** word.

_____

Name _____

✿ **Trace and write.**

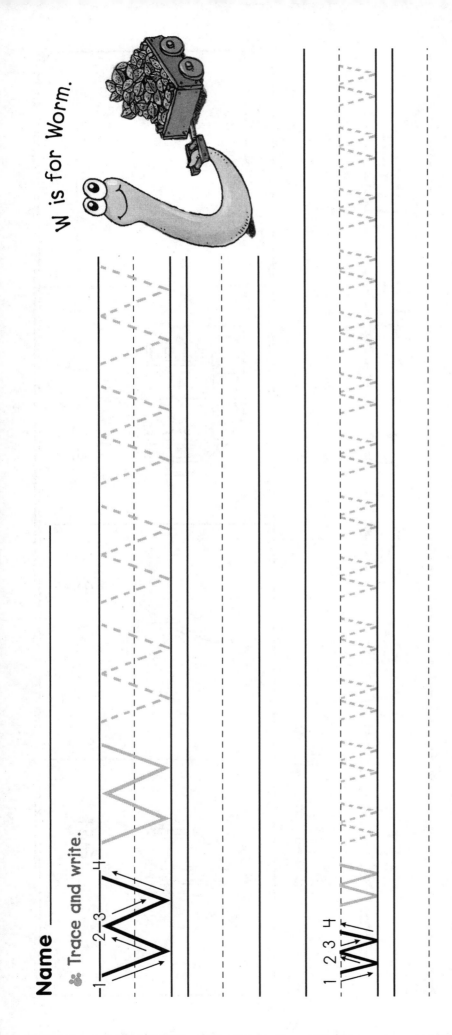

W is for Worm.

✿ **Circle every W and every w.**

W	V	M	V	U	W	V	M	W	M	V
w	v	v	u	m	w	w	w	v	m	u

I found _____ W's and _____ w's.

Name _____

✤ Trace the W and w.

W orm had a W agon.

✤ Now write the W and w.

___orm had a ___agon.

✤ Add w's and then read the words.

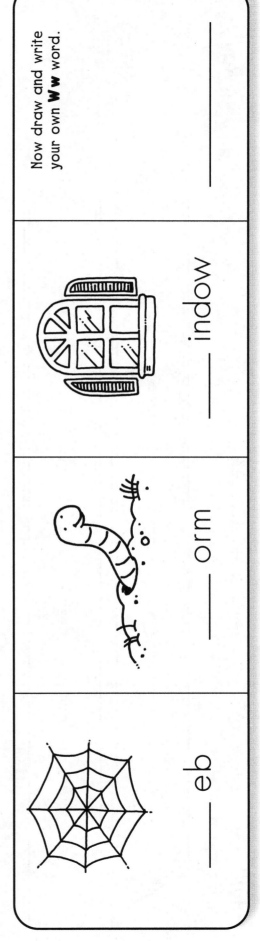

___eb

___orm

___indow

Now draw and write your own **Ww** word.

_____

Name _____

✎ Trace and write.

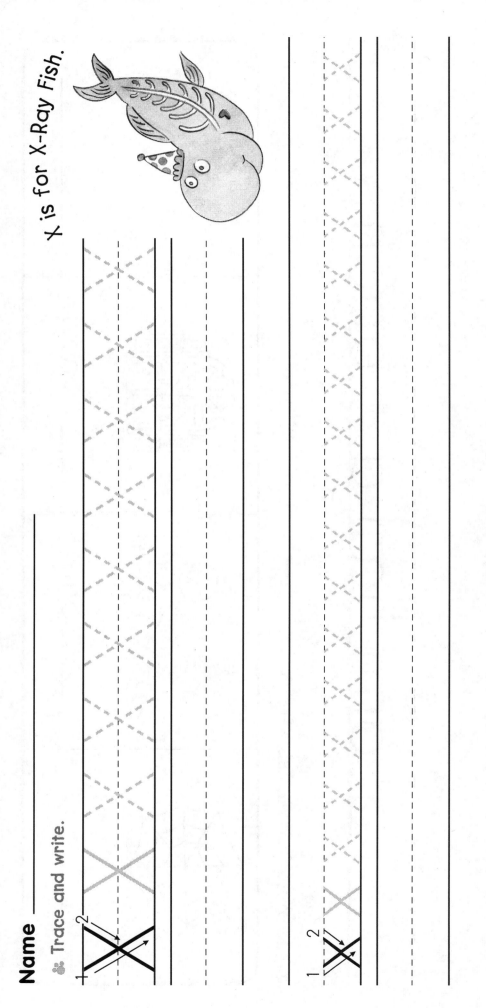

X is for X-Ray Fish.

✿ Circle every X and every x.

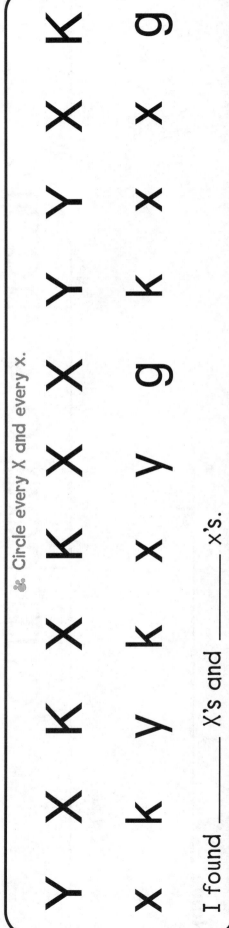

Y	X	K	K	X	Y	Y	X	K
x	k	k	y	k	x	y	g	k	x	g

I found _____ X's and _____ x's.

Name _____

❀ Trace the X and x.

X -Ray fish plays Xylophone.

❀ Now write the X and x.

_ -Ray fish plays _ ylophone.

❀ Add x's and then read the words.

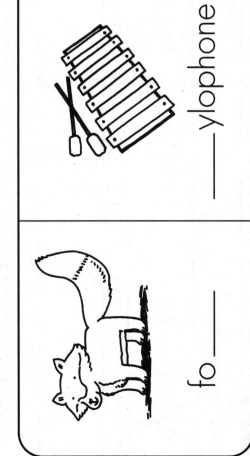

fo _ _

____ ylophone

____ -ray

Now draw and write your own **X x** word.

____

Name _____

Y is for Yak.

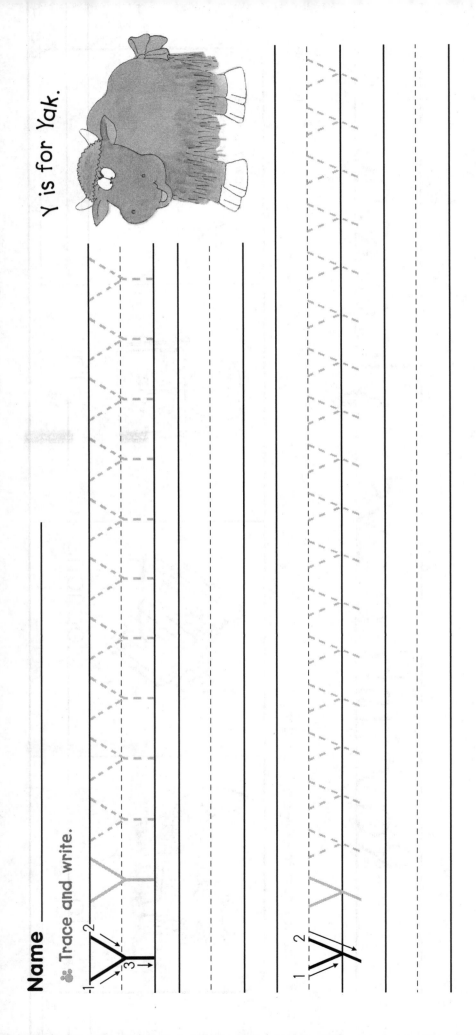

✺ Trace and write.

✺ Circle every Y and every y.

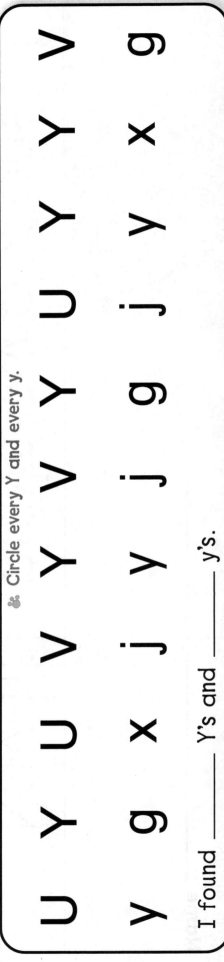

I found _____ Y's and _____ y's.

Name _____

✤ Trace the y's.

The ¹Yak ate ¹Yogurt.

✤ Now write the y's.

The _ak ate _ogurt.

✤ Add y's and then read the words.

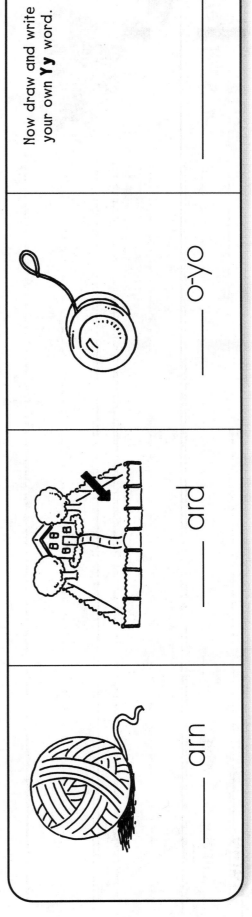

_____ arn

_____ ard

_____ o-yo

Now draw and write your own **Y y** word.

_____

Name _____

✿ Trace and write.

Z is for Zebra.

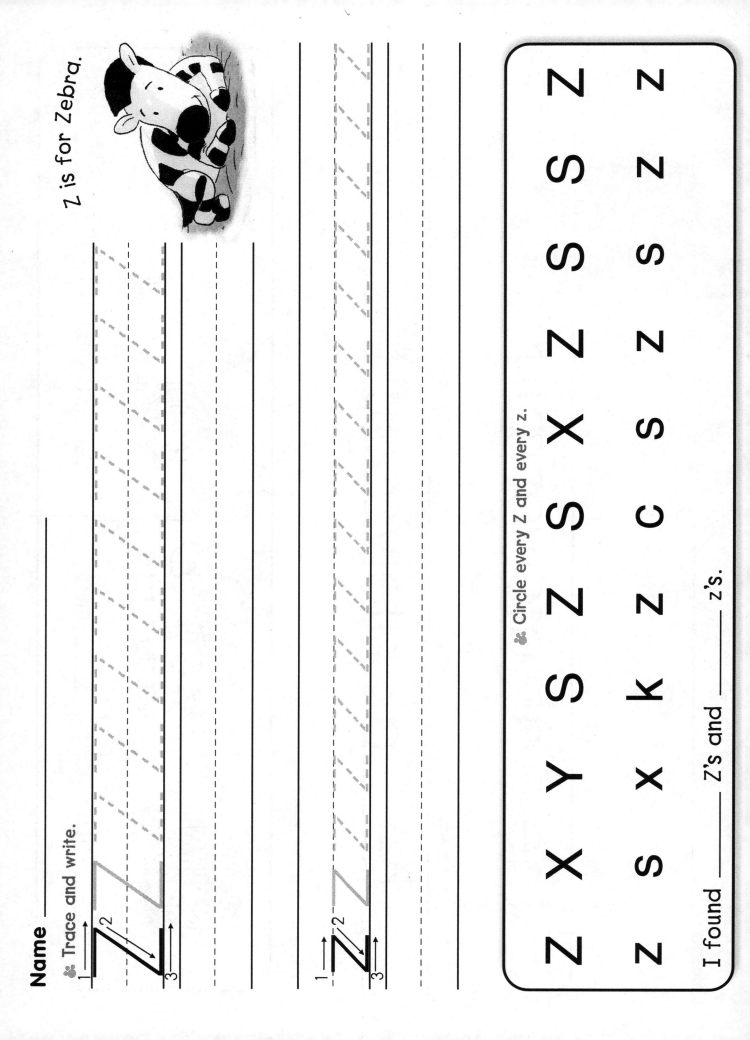

✿ Circle every Z and every z.

Z	X	Y	S	Z	S	X	Z	S
z	s	x	k	z	c	s	z	z

I found _____ Z's and _____ z's.

Name _____

✿ Trace the Z's and z's.

The Zebra lives at the Zoo.

✿ Now write the Z's and z's.

The ___ebra lives at the ___oo.

✿ Add z's and then read the words.

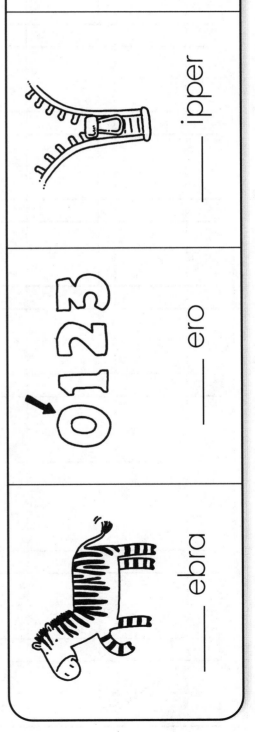

___ ebra

0123 ___ ero

___ ipper

Now draw and write your own **Z z** word.

_____

Now that I know my ABC's,
Here's a letter to you from me!

My ABC Mini-Book
An Alphabet of Animals

by _____

Aa

Bb

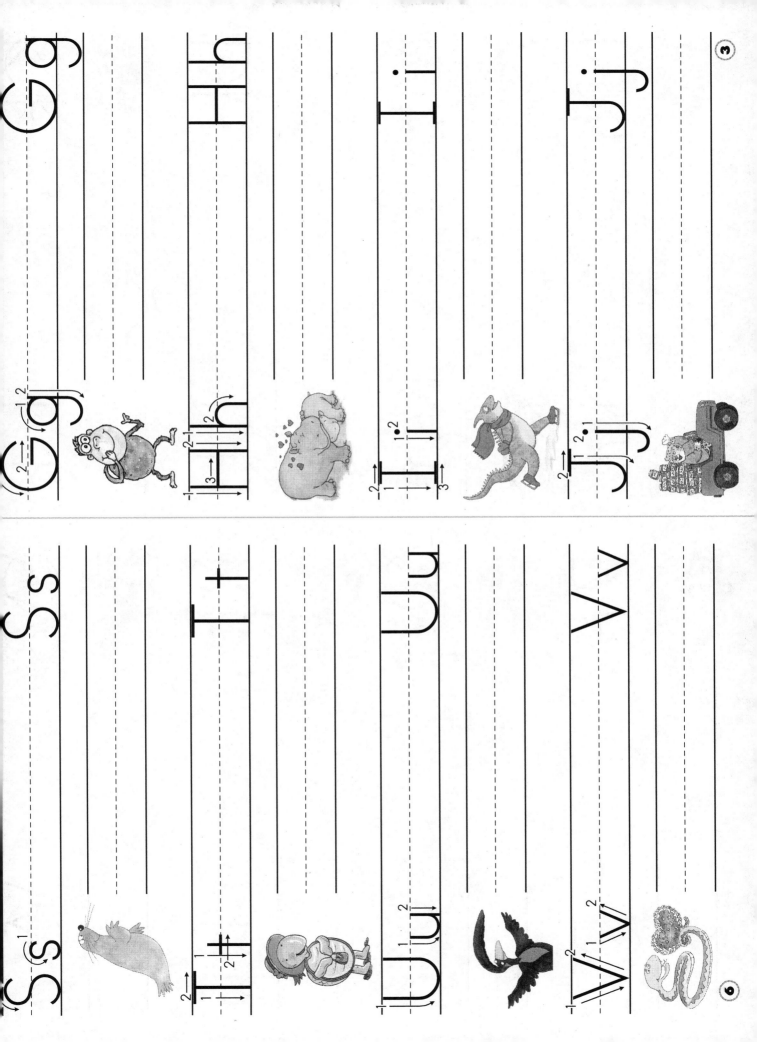

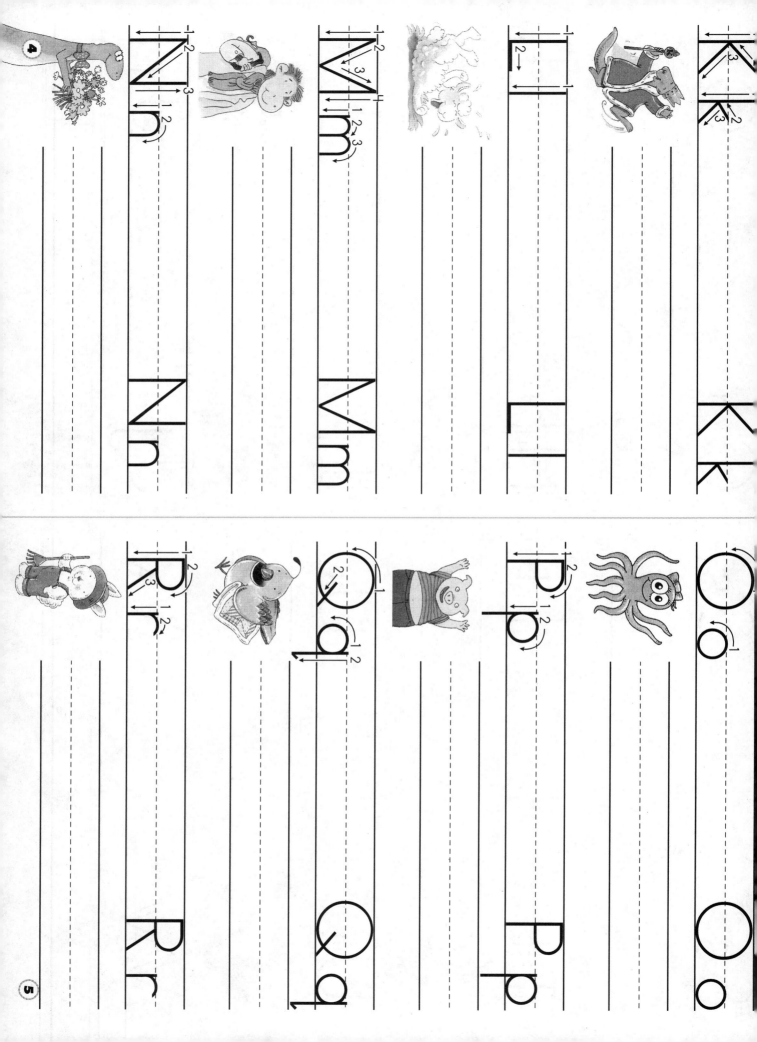